PIANO • VOCAL • GUITAR

SONGS OF THE 30's

THE DECADE SERIES

D1398400

HAL•LEONARD™
CORPORATION

7777 W. BLUEMOUND RD. P.O. BOX 13819 MILWAUKEE, WI 53213

SONGS OF THE 30's

THE DECADE SERIES

Contents

THE THIRTIES

by Stanley Green

HINDENBURG EXPLODES
33 Killed, 64 Saved in Lakehurst Blas

$\mathcal{I}$f ever a decade needed songs to lift its spirits and send it spinning merrily across a dance floor, that decade was the Thirties. From the Wall Street crash to the outbreak of World War II, it was a period marked by the Great Depression at home and darkening war clouds abroad. This, then, was the era of soup kitchens, breadlines and bank failures, of bonus marchers and dust storms, of painful labor gains and rampant lawless gangs. Overseas, a far more menacing form of rampant lawlessness was evident. Under Nazi Führer Adolf Hitler, German troops

occupied the Rhineland and scooped up Austria and Czechoslovakia. Under Fascist Duce Benito Mussolini, Italian forces subdued Ethiopia and Albania. Under the Japanese war lords, soldiers of the Empire of the Rising Sun subjugated Manchuria and other vast areas of China. At the decade's end, when Hitler and Soviet dictator Joseph Stalin agreed to carve up Poland between them, virtually the entire planet was plunged into the havoc of the most devastating conflict in history.

*Adolph Hitler driving
into Austria*

$\mathcal{T}$he Thirties also had its share of other tragic headlines to take people's minds off their own imminent and potential troubles. In 1932, the 19-month-old baby of aviation ace Charles Lindbergh and Anne Morrow Lindbergh was kidnapped and murdered. In 1934, the S. S. Morro Castle went down in flames near Asbury Park, New Jersey, with a loss of over 125 lives. In 1937, the zeppelin Hindenburg, the world's largest dirigible, crashed on landing at Lakehurst, New Jersey, with a loss of 33 lives. No event, however, so intrigued a gossip-hungry public than the decision, in 1936, of Britain's King Edward VIII to abdicate the throne to marry American divorcée Wallis Warfield Simpson.

'I Am David Windsor'

$\mathcal{B}$ut despite roadblocks, it was still possible in the Thirties for people to cross over to the sunny side of the street. Prohibition was repealed. Franklin D. Roosevelt was in the White House energizing a dispirited nation with his alphabetical New Deal programs (NRA, CCC, PWA, WPA) and his broadcast fireside chats. Gable, Crawford, Garbo, and Shirley Temple were on the silver screen, Joe Louis was in the ring, Lou Gehrig was up at bat, "Wrong-Way" Corrigan was up in the air, and the Dionne Quintuplets were in their bassinets. The period also had its share of nonsense in the form of goldfish swallowing, zoot suits, and the game of knock-knock. ("Knock-knock." "Who's there?" "Machiavelli." "Machiavelli who?" "Machiavelli good suit for $40.")

Roosevelt and His First Cabinet

*A*s far as music was concerned, the Thirties was the decade of the big bands. They could be sweet or swingy, tasteful or gimmicky, but each orchestra had its own distinctive sound and style. Tootling a clarinet (like Benny Goodman and Artie Shaw), or blowing through a trombone (like Tommy Dorsey and Glenn Miller), or just waving a stick (like Guy Lombardo and Sammy Kaye), the band leaders were latter-day Pied Pipers luring millions into dance halls, movie palaces, nightclubs, and college proms. Even unseen — thanks to radio and recordings — they moved right into the nation's parlors and bedrooms, generating a musical excitement that did much to help people escape from the seemingly unmanagable conditions of the world.

*A*nd what an array of personalities and songs there were. Offering "The Sweetest Music This Side of Heaven," Guy Lombardo and his Royal Canadians were on hand to bounce through the tearstained cry of the spurned lover called "Boo-Hoo," or to glide along to the beat of "Heartaches." Nasal-voiced Rudy Vallee and his Connecticut Yankees managed to sail

smoothly through the misty "Harbor Lights." Glen Gray and the Casa Loma Orchestra — with Sonny Dunham on trumpet — could be heard recalling fond "Memories of You." The languid romantic appeal of the South, both astral and lunar, was captured by the orchestras of Jack Teagarden in "Stars Fell on Alabama" and Ted Fiorito in "Moon Over Miami." Another "moon" song — "Moonglow" — was written by bandleaders Will Hudson and Eddie DeLange as a specialty for their own Hudson-DeLange Orchestra. Songs of foreign origin also won favor in the Thirties when introduced in the United States by leading dance bands. From France came "Avant de Mourir," better known as "My Prayer," which was popularized by

Glenn Miller and His Orchestra

orchestra and "I Can't Get Started" (a show tune by Vernon Duke and Ira Gershwin) became both his theme and biggest selling record.

As the decade came to a close, Glenn Miller emerged with his orchestra and first resounding hit, "In the Mood." (Remember the windup with the members of the brass section facing in all directions as they repeated the riff over and over again?) Even closer to jazz roots were the orchestras of two composer-pianists, the exuberant Fats Waller (who did *not* compose his most popular number, "I'm Gonna Sit Right Down and Write Myself a Letter"), and the more urbane Duke Ellington (whose standards include "Caravan" and "Mood Indigo").

Cab Calloway

Sammy Kaye's Swing and Sway group; from Cuba, "Para Vego Me Voy," which became "Say Si Si" when it was brought over by rhumba maestro Xavier Cugat; and from Mexico, "Cuando Vuelva a Tu Lado" — or "What a Diff'rence a Day Made" — was identified with Richard Himber's Ritz-Carlton Orchestra.

*I*n 1934, Benny Goodman organized his first dance band and within two years had been proclaimed the undisputed King of Swing. Like every orchestra at the time, Goodman's had a theme song, the bright, crisp invitation, "Let's Dance." Another theme song, "I'm Getting Sentimental Over You," became the trade mark of that Sentimental Gentleman of Swing, Tommy Dorsey. Dorsey also had a resounding hit — with young Frank Sinatra on the vocals — when he introduced the threnodic "I'll Never Smile Again," penned by pianist Ruth Lowe in memory of her husband who had died within a year after their marriage. In 1937, Dorsey's star trumpeter, Bunny Berigan, left the band to front his own

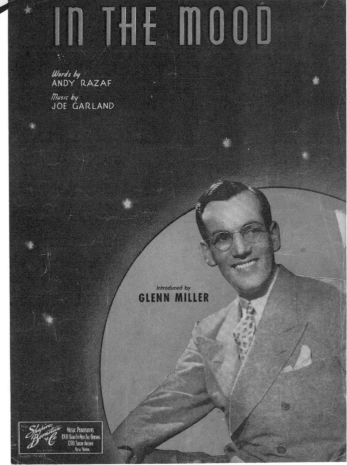

IN THE MOOD

Words by
ANDY RAZAF
Music by
JOE GARLAND

Introduced by
GLENN MILLER

George Gershwin

Goldwyn Follies. Another major figure of the American musical theatre was Cole Porter, who wrote both music and lyrics for two Hollywood spectacles of 1936 — *Born to Dance,* which introduced "Easy to Love" (sung by James Stewart to Eleanor Powell), and *Rosalie,* which introduced "In the Still of the Night" (sung by Nelson Eddy to Eleanor Powell).

The most popular singing idol of the screen, however, was the former Paul Whiteman vocalist, Bing Crosby, who casually crooned his way through 24 movies during the decade. One of these, *Pennies from Heaven,* gave us a title song that philosophically urged the acceptance of bad times in order to be able to enjoy good times ("If you want the things you love, you must have showers"). On the technical front, surely among the great innovations in the art of the cinema was *Snow White and the Seven Dwarfs,* Walt Disney's first full-length animated cartoon, whose score included the poignant "Someday My Prince Will Come."

The incredible appeal of the "talkies" did much to bring about the demise of vaudeville as the most popular form of mass entertainment. Songs, of course, quickly became a major attraction on the screen — whether they were sung by Ruby and Dick in backstage sagas, Fred and Ginger in glossy comic escapades, or Jeanette and Nelson in romantic costume epics. These musicals called upon the services of the top talent of both Hollywood and Broadway. In 1934, "The Continental," by Con Conrad and Herb Magidson, was introduced in the Astaire-Rogers vehicle *The Gay Divorcee* and became the first song to win an Academy Award. Three years later, George and Ira Gershwin contributed the score for the team's seventh movie, *Shall We Dance,* in which Fred sang the rueful admission "They Can't Take That Away From Me." The songwriting brothers followed up that movie with *A Damsel in Distress,* Astaire's first solo starring movie, whence came "Nice Work if You Can Get It" and "A Foggy Day." The last song George Gershwin wrote before his untimely death at the age of 38 was "Love Is Here to Stay," included in his score for The

Fred Astaire

After rapid growth in the Twenties, radio became the major provider of home entertainment in the Thirties. The coverage was now broad enough to include news events, comedy programs (Jack Benny, Amos and Andy), dramas (in 1938, Orson Welles scared the pants off gullible listeners with his dramatization of H. G. Wells' *The War of the Worlds*), and musical variety shows. Among those whose voices introduced and popularized songs over the air were Bing Crosby (singing his theme "Where the Blue of the Night Meets the Gold of the Day"), dynamic Belle Baker ("All of Me"), Irish tenor Morton Downey ("For All We Know"), and Crosby's chief crooning rivals, Rudy Vallee ("Nevertheless") and Russ Columbo ("Love Letters in the Sand").

The Broadway theatre of the Thirties, though hardly as robust as it had been during the halcyon days of the previous decade, still managed to offer many successful shows and durable songs. And once again it was blessed by contributions from the giants of American music — Jerome Kern, Irving Berlin, George Gershwin, Richard Rodgers, and Cole Porter. Kern, generally acknowledged as the father of musical comedy joined lyricist Otto Harbach to provide a rich, melodic score for *Roberta,* including the brooding torch ballad "Smoke Gets in Your Eyes." In 1935, Gershwin, in collaboration with his brother Ira and DuBose Heyward, created the classic folk opera, *Porgy and Bess,* in which the plaintive lullaby "Summertime" was first heard. After spending over two years in Hollywood, Rodgers and his partner Lorenz Hart returned to Broadway in the mid-Thirties for a succession of hits such as *Babes in Arms,* featuring "The Lady Is a Tramp," "Where or When," and "My Funny Valentine," and *The Boys from Syracuse,* featuring "Falling in Love With Love" and "This Can't Be Love." And Porter continued

*Tamara Sings
"Smoke Gets In Your Eyes"*

Richard Rodgers and Lorenz Hart

Jerome Kern

to transport audiences into his own glittering, carefree world with a total of nine musicals, including *Red, Hot and Blue!* In that one, Ethel Merman and Bob Hope sang the duet "It's DeLovely," relating the story of a girl and boy from the night they fall in love, through their wedding and honeymoon, and up to the birth of their first born.

*J*oining the ranks of Broadway masters in the Thirties was Kurt Weill, a victim of Hitler's Germany, who quickly became a leader in expanding the horizons of the commercial musical theatre. Weill's second Broadway show, *Knickerbocker Holiday,* written with Maxwell Anderson, not only provided Walter Huston (as Pieter Stuyvesant) with the memorable "September Song," it also showed deep concern for the vital issue of freedom versus totalitarianism. This, in fact, was the issue that — on September 3, 1939 — at last rallied the European democracies to strike back at Hitler's aggression. Only twenty years after "the war to end war," another even more horrible carnage had begun.

Walter Huston as Pieter Stuyvesant

Kurt Weill

Ethel Merman and Bob Hope in "Red, Hot and Blue!"

ALL OF ME

By SEYMOUR SIMONS
and GERALD MARKS

13

BLUE PRELUDE

Words by GORDON JENKINS
Music by JOE BISHOP

BOO-HOO

Words and Music by EDWARD HEYMAN,
CARMEN LOMBARDO and JOHN JACOB LOEB

BYE BYE BLUES

By FRED HAMM, DAVE BENNETT,
BERT LOWN, CHAUNCEY GRAY

THE CONTINENTAL

Words by HERBERT MAGIDSON
Music by CON CONRAD

find,_____ while you're danc-ing,_____ That there's a

rhy-thm in your heart and soul;_ A cer-tain rhy-thm that you can't con-trol,_ And you will

do "The Con-ti-nen-tal" all_ the time._____

Beau-ti-ful mu-sic!_____

Dan-ger-ous rhy-thm!_____

CARAVAN

By DUKE ELLINGTON,
IRVING MILLS & JUAN TIZOL

This _____ is so ex - cit - - ing _____

You _____ are so in - vit - - ing _____

Rest - - ing in my arms _____ As I

thrill to the mag - ic charms _____ of

EAST OF THE SUN
(And West Of The Moon)

Slowly, With Expression

Words and Music by
BROOKS BOWMAN

EASY TO LOVE

(From "BORN TO DANCE")

Words and Music by COLE PORTER

FALLING IN LOVE WITH LOVE
(From "THE BOYS FROM SYRACUSE")

Words by LORENZ HART
Music by RICHARD RODGERS

A FOGGY DAY

(From "A DAMSEL IN DISTRESS")

Words by IRA GERSHWIN
Music by GEORGE GERSHWIN

FOR ALL WE KNOW

Words by SAM M. LEWIS
Music by J. FRED COOTS

HARBOR LIGHTS

Words and Music by
JIMMY KENNEDY and HUGH WILLIAMS

HAVE YOU EVER BEEN LONELY?
(HAVE YOU EVER BEEN BLUE?)

Words by GEORGE BROWN
Music by PETER DEROSE

1. Two of a kind___ ev'-ry-where I see Lov-ers in the moon-light, rob-ins in a tree
2. My hap-pi-ness___ two a-lone can share Now that I have lost you, life is hard to bear

Now that we have part-ed what am I to do But make this plea to
You and I have quar-reled I'm a fool, it's true Why can't we start a-

you: Have you ev-er been lone - ly?___ Have you ev-er been
new:

8va- - - ⌡

I CAN'T GET STARTED

(From "ZIEGFELD FOLLIES OF 1936")

Words by IRA GERSHWIN
Music by VERNON DUKE

"Su - per - man Turns Out To Be Flash In The Pan!"

I've flown a - round the world_ in a plane;_____ I've set - tled re - vo - lu - tions in
(I do a) hun - dred yards_ in ten flat;_____ The Prince of Wales has cop - ied my

Spain;_____ The North Pole I have char - ted, But can't get start - ed with you.____
hat;_____ With queens I've â la cart - ed, But can't get start - ed with you.____

A - round a golf course I'm un - der par,_____ And all the mov - ies want_ me to
The lead - ing tail - ors fol - low my styles,_____ And tooth-paste ads all fea - ture my

HEARTACHES

Words by JOHN KLENNER
Music by AL HOFFMAN

Lyrics:
You said you loved me just as I love you, ____
And I be-lieved it all; _____

MCA MUSIC

I DON'T KNOW WHY
(I JUST DO)

Words by ROY TURK
Music by FRED E. AHLERT

Slowly, with feeling

I'LL NEVER SMILE AGAIN

Words and Music by
RUTH LOWE

MCA MUSIC

I'M GETTING SENTIMENTAL OVER YOU

Words by NED WASHINGTON
Music by GEORGE BASSMAN

I'M GONNA SIT RIGHT DOWN AND WRITE MYSELF A LETTER

Words by JOE YOUNG
Music by FRED E. AHLERT

I'VE GOT THE WORLD ON A STRING

(From "Cotton Club Parade - 21st Edition")

Tune Ukulele

G C E A

Lyric by TED KOEHLER
Music by HAROLD ARLEN

Moderato

Bell Vamp

Mer-ry month of May, sun-ny skies of blue, clouds have rolled a-way and the sun peeps thru, May ex-press ____ hap-pi-ness, ____ Joy you may de-fine in a thous-and ways, but a case like mine needs a "spe-cial phrase" to re-veal ____ how I feel. ____

CHORUS

I've got the world on a string,— sit-tin' on a rain-bow, Got the string a-round my fin-

—ger, What a world, what a life,— I'm in love! I've got a

song that I sing,— I can make the rain go, an-y time I move my fin - - ger,

Luck-y me, can't you see, I'm in love,— Life is a beau-ti-ful thing,—

I'VE GOT YOU UNDER MY SKIN
(From "BORN TO DANCE")

Words and Music by COLE PORTER

I've got you _____ un-der my skin, _____

I've got you _____ deep in the

heart of me, _____ So deep in my heart, _____

IN A SHANTY IN OLD SHANTY TOWN

Words by JOE YOUNG
Music by LITTLE JACK LITTLE and JOHN SIRAS

Valse Moderato

Lyrics:
I'm up in the world, But I'd give the world, To be where I used to be; A heav-en-ly nest, Where I rest the best, Means more than the world to me.

IN THE MOOD

Words and Music by JOE GARLAND

Who's the liv-in' dol-ly with the beau-ti-ful eyes___ What a pair o' lips, I'd like to

try 'em for size___ I'll just tell her, "Ba-by, won't you swing it with me"___

IT AIN'T NECESSARILY SO

Words by IRA GERSHWIN
Music by GEORGE GERSHWIN

Tempo I

Jo - nah, he lived in de whale,   Oh, Jo - nah, he lived in de
Mo - ses was found in a stream,   Li'l Mo - ses was found in a

whale,   Fo' he made his home in Dat fish -'s ab - do - men. Oh,
stream,   He float - ed on wa - ter Till Ole Phar - aoh's daugh - ter She

Jo - nah, he lived in de   whale._____   Li'l
fished him, she says, from that   stream.

Allegro

Wa - doo,__ All: Wa - doo,__ SP.L.: Zim bam bod - dle - oo, Zim bam bod - dle - oo, Hoo - dle ah da wa da,

IT'S A BLUE WORLD

Words and Music by
BOB WRIGHT and CHET FORREST

IT'S DE-LOVELY

(From "RED, HOT AND BLUE!")

Words and Music by
COLE PORTER

*Pronounced "delukes"

IT'S ONLY A PAPER MOON

Words by BILLY ROSE and E.Y. HARBURG
Music by HAROLD ARLEN

Say, It's On-ly A Pa-per Moon, Sail-ing o-ver a card-board sea,

But it would-n't be make be-lieve, If you be-lieved in me.

Yes, it's on-ly a can-vas sky, Hang-ing o-ver a mus-lin tree,

IT'S THE TALK OF THE TOWN

Words by MARTY SYMES
and A.J. NEIBURG
Music by JERRY LIVINGSTON

Slowly, with expression

IN THE STILL OF THE NIGHT
(From "ROSALIE")

Moderately

Words and Music by COLE PORTER

LOVE IS HERE TO STAY

(From GOLDWYN FOLLIES)

Words by IRA GERSHWIN
Music by GEORGE GERSHWIN

THE LADY IS A TRAMP
(From "BABES IN ARMS")

Words by LORENZ HART
Music by RICHARD RODGERS

LET'S DANCE

Words and Music by
FANNY BALDRIDGE, GREGORY STONE
and JOSEPH BONIME

LOVE LETTERS IN THE SAND

Words by NICK KENNY
and CHARLES KENNY
Music by J. FRED COOTS

Moderato

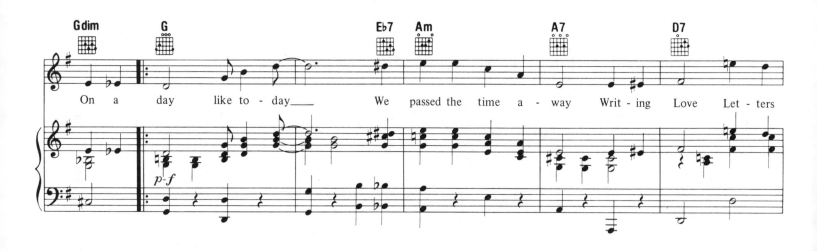

On a day like to-day___ We passed the time a-way Writ-ing Love Let-ters

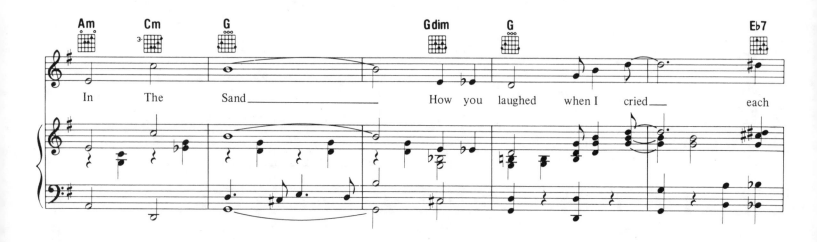

In The Sand___ How you laughed when I cried___ each

LULLABY OF THE LEAVES

Words by JOE YOUNG
Music by BERNICE PETKERE

MEMORIES OF YOU

Words by ANDY RAZAF
Music by EUBIE BLAKE

MOOD INDIGO

Words and Music by DUKE ELLINGTON,
ALBANY BIGARD and IRVING MILLS

MOONGLOW

By WILL HUDSON,
EDDIE DELANGE & IRVING MILLS

MOON OVER MIAMI

Words by EDGAR LESLIE
Music by JOE BURKE

MY FUNNY VALENTINE

(From "BABES IN ARMS")

Words by LORENZ HART
Music by RICHARD RODGERS

MY PRAYER

Music by GEORGES BOULANGER
Lyric and Musical Adaptation by JIMMY KENNEDY

NEVERTHELESS
(I'm In Love With You)

Words and Music by
BERT KALMAR and HARRY RUBY

Moderately Slow, With Expression

May-be I'm right,__ and may-be I'm wrong,__ And may-be I'm weak,__ and may-be I'm strong:__ But

Nev-er-the-less,__ I'm In Love With You.

May-be I'll win__ and may-be I'll lose,__ And may-be I'm in;__ for cry-in' the blues:__ But

NICE WORK IF YOU CAN GET IT

(From "A DAMSEL IN DISTRESS")

Words by IRA GERSHWIN
Music by GEORGE GERSHWIN

The man who on-ly lives for mak-ing mon-ey Lives a life that is-n't nec-es-sa-ri-ly sun-ny. Like-wise the man who works for fame, There's no guar-an-tee that time won't e-rase his name.

ON THE SUNNY SIDE OF THE STREET

Lyric by DOROTHY FIELDS
Music by JIMMY McHUGH

PAPER DOLL

By JOHNNY S. BLACK

PENNIES FROM HEAVEN

Words by JOHN BURKE
Music by ARTHUR JOHNSTON

STARS FELL ON ALABAMA

Words by MITCHELL PARISH
Music by FRANK PERKINS

RED SAILS IN THE SUNSET

Words by JIMMY KENNEDY
Music by HUGH WILLIAMS

SAY "SI, SI"

Music by ERNESTO LECUONA
Spanish Words by FRANCIA LUBAN
English Words by AL STILLMAN

Here's a lit-tle know - ledge _____ Quite good _____
Va - mos a la con - ga _____ Ay Dios _____

May - be it won't help you _____ But it should _____
Va - mos que ya sue - na _____ El bon - go _____

155

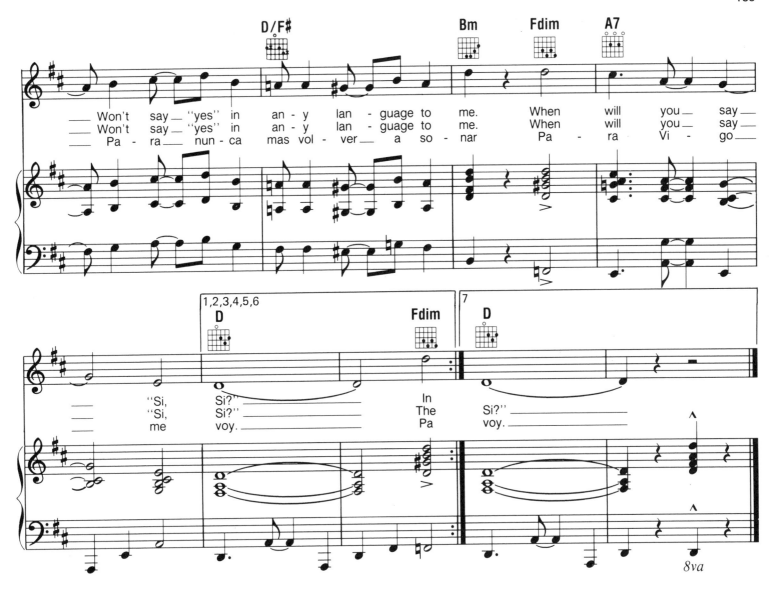

3rd Chorus
The monkeys in the tree
Don't have to say: "Si, Si";
All they do is wag their little tails;
That's a little gag that never fails.
In darkest Africa
The natives say: "Uh, Huh!"
But you never hear my plea,
Won't say "Yes" in any language to me
When will you say: "Si, Si"?

5th Chorus
In Washington, D.C.,
The yes-men say: "Si, Si";
There are lots of politicians, though
Who can always say both "Yes" and "No"
But sweetheart tell me why,
No matter how I try,
You won't listen to my plea
Won't say "Yes" in any language to me
When will you say "Si Si"?

4th Chorus
Out West they say: "Wah Hoo!"
That's "O.K., Toots" to you.
Every Southern lady knows her stuff,
'Cause her answer always is "Sho Nuff!"
But, sweetheart, tell me why,
No matter how I try,
You won't listen to my plea,
Won't say "Yes" in any language to me
When will you say: "Si, Si"?

6th Chorus
A lady horse, they say,
Means "Yes" when she says: "Neigh!"
Every little gal from Mexico
Hates to give a pal a "No, No, No!"
So, sweetheart, tell me why,
No matter how I try,
You won't listen to my plea
Won't say "Yes" in any language to me
When will you say "Si Si"?

7th Chorus
In 606 B.C.,
Those gals would mix, Si, Si!
Every little cave man used his dome,
Hit 'em on the head, then dragged 'em home.
So, sweetheart, tell me why,
No matter how I try,
You won't listen to my plea
Won't say "Yes" in any language to me,
When will you say: Si, Si"?

SEPTEMBER SONG
(From the Musical Play "KNICKERBOCKER HOLIDAY")

Words by MAXWELL ANDERSON
Music by KURT WEILL

SMOKE GETS IN YOUR EYES
(From "ROBERTA")

Words by OTTO HARBACH
Music by JEROME KERN

(From "Snow White And The Seven Dwarfs")

SOME DAY MY PRINCE WILL COME
(Someday I'll Find My Love)

Words by LARRY MOREY
Music by FRANK CHURCHILL

SUMMERTIME

(From "PORGY AND BESS")

Words by DuBOSE HEYWARD
Music by GEORGE GERSHWIN

THAT'S MY DESIRE

Words by CARROLL LOVEDAY
Music by HELMY KRESA

THESE FOOLISH THINGS
(REMIND ME OF YOU)

Words by HOLT MARVELL
Music by JACK STRACHEY and HARRY LINK

THEY CAN'T TAKE THAT AWAY FROM ME

Words by IRA GERSHWIN
Music by GEORGE GERSHWIN

With movement

Our ro-mance won't end on a sor-row-ful note, Though by to-mor-row you're

gone;____ The song is end-ed, but as the song-writ-er wrote, The

mel-o-dy ling-ers on. They may take you from me, I'll miss your fond ca-

UNDER A BLANKET OF BLUE

Words by MARTY SYMES and AL J. NEIBURG
Music by JERRY LIVINGSTON

THIS CAN'T BE LOVE
(From "THE BOYS FROM SYRACUSE")

Words by LORENZ HART
Music by RICHARD RODGERS

WHAT A DIFF'RENCE A DAY MADE

Lyric by STANLEY ADAMS
Music by MARIA GREVER

WHERE OR WHEN
(From "BABES IN ARMS")

Words by LORENZ HART
Music by RICHARD RODGERS

YOU'RE MY EVERYTHING

Words by MORT DIXON and JOE YOUNG
Music by HARRY WARREN

YOURS

Words by ALBERT GAMSE and JACK SHERR
Music by GONZALO ROIG

WHERE THE BLUE OF THE NIGHT
(Meets The Gold Of The Day)

Words and Music by
ROY TURK, BING CROSBY
and FRED E. AHLERT

Moderate

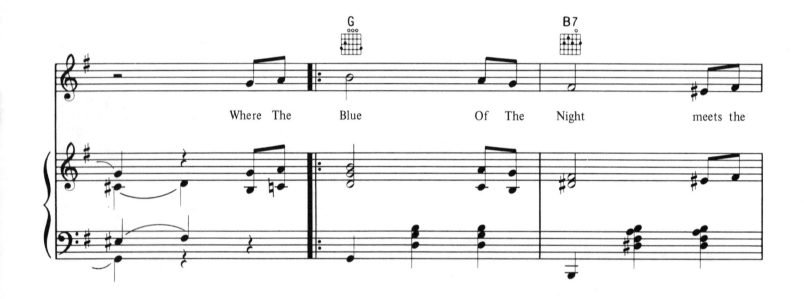

Where The Blue Of The Night meets the

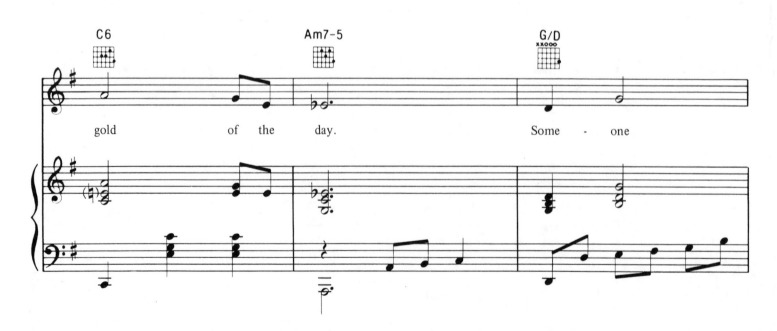

gold of the day. Some-one